FOR ORGANS, PIANOS & ELECTRONIC KEYBOARDS

E Z PLAY TODAY ®

312

BARBRA
Love is the answer

Photography by Firooz Zahedi, www.firoozzahedi.com

T0056177

ISBN: 978-1-60378-244-9

E-Z Play® Today Music Notation © 1975 by HAL LEONARD CORPORATION

E-Z PLAY and EASY ELECTRONIC KEYBOARD MUSIC are registered trademarks of HAL LEONARD CORPORATION.

Visit our website at www.cherrylaneprint.com

Here's to Life

Registration 3
Rhythm: Ballad

Music by Artie Butler
Lyrics by Phyllis Molinary

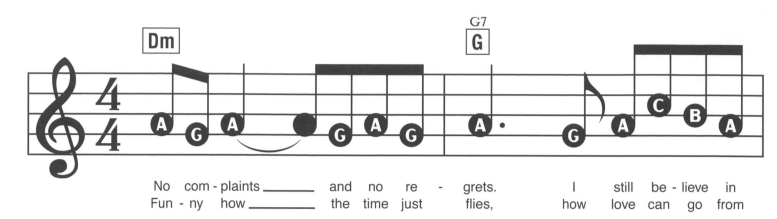

No com - plaints _____ and no re - grets. I still be - lieve in
Fun - ny how _____ the time just flies, how love can go from

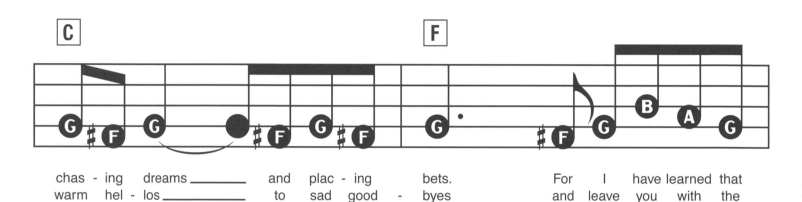

chas - ing dreams _____ and plac - ing bets. For I have learned that
warm hel - los _____ to sad good - byes and leave you with the

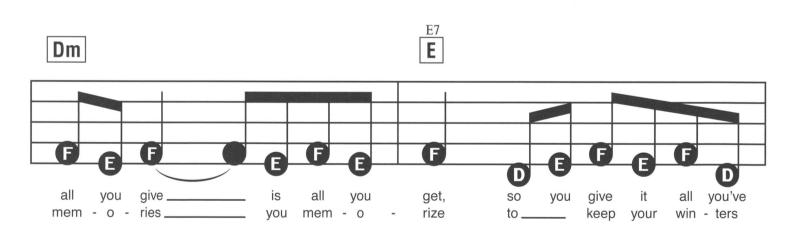

all you give _____ is all you get, so you give it all you've
mem - o - ries _____ you mem - o - rize to _____ keep your win - ters

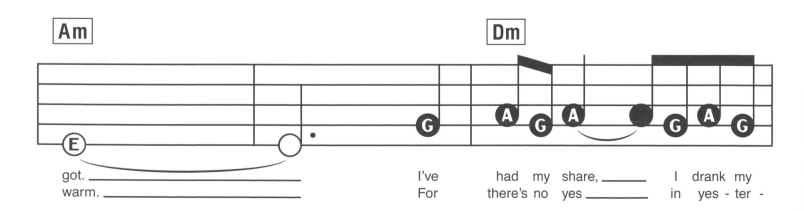

got. _____ I've had my share, _____ I drank my
warm. _____ For there's no yes _____ in yes - ter -

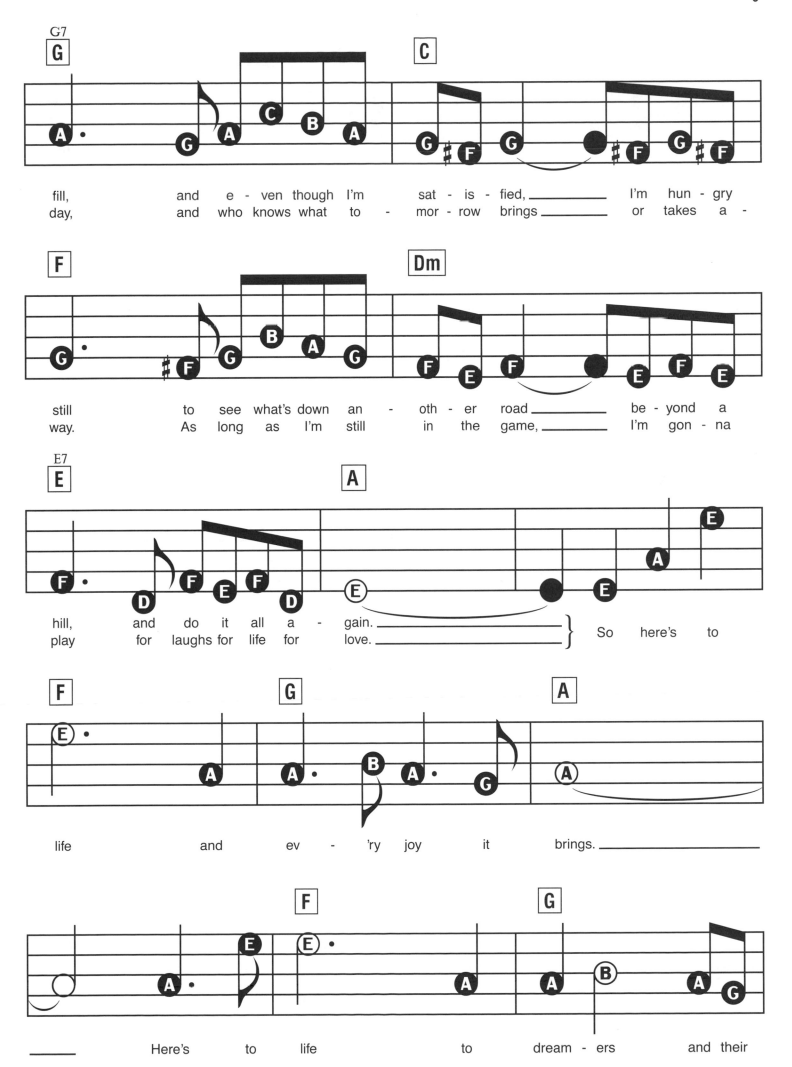

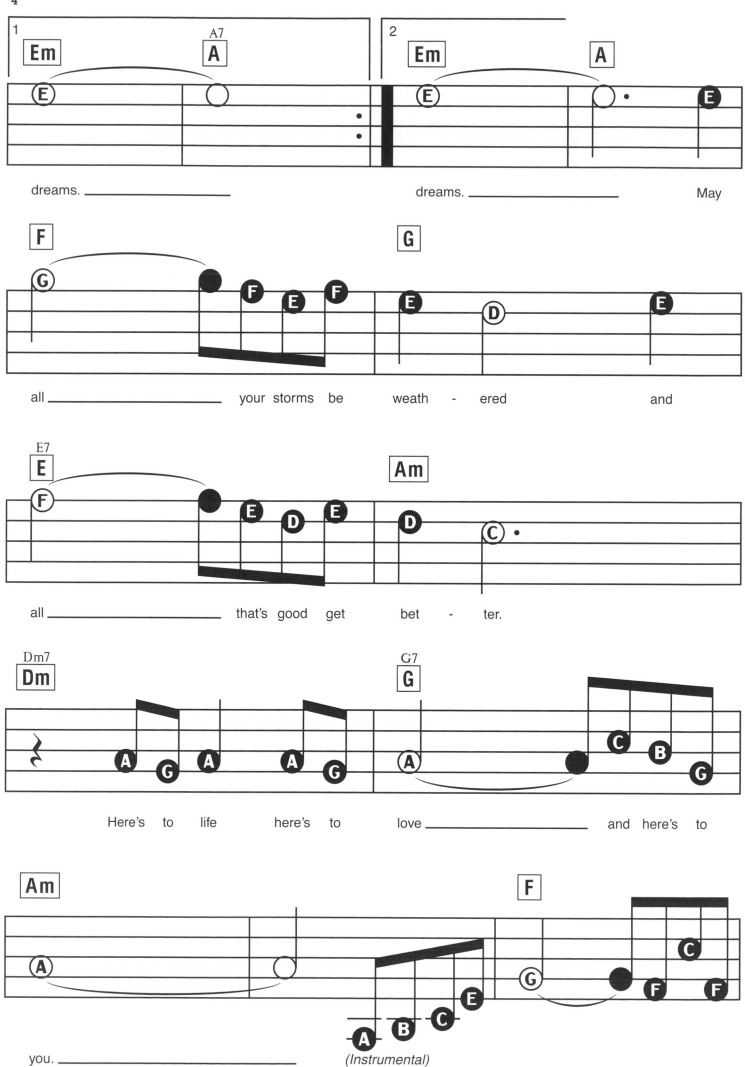

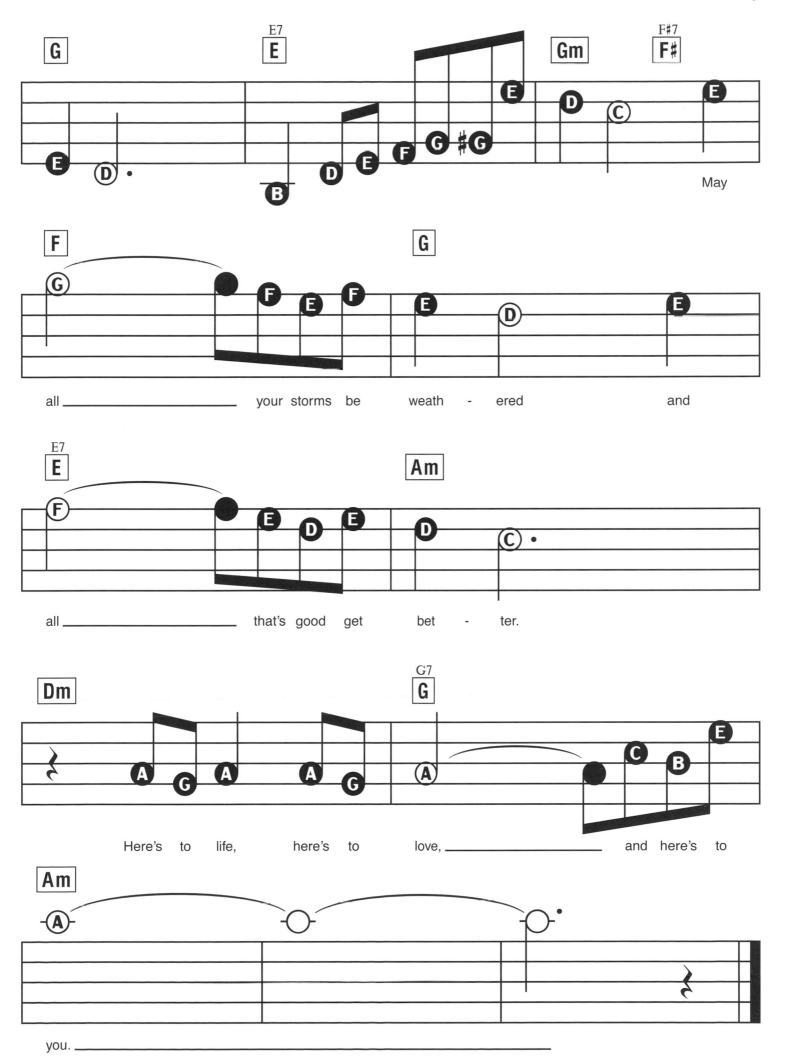

In the Wee Small Hours of the Morning

Registration 2
Rhythm: Ballad

Words by Bob Hilliard
Music by David Mann

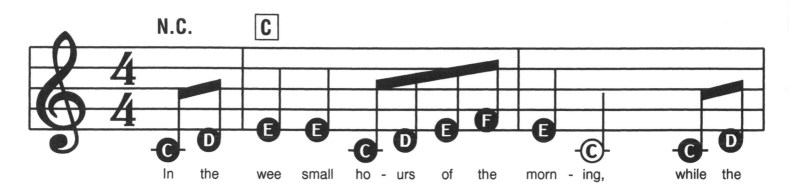

In the wee small ho - urs of the morn - ing, while the

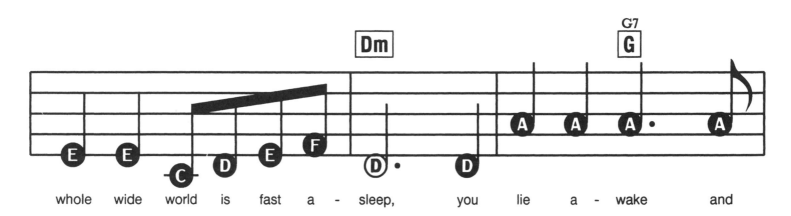

whole wide world is fast a - sleep, you lie a - wake and

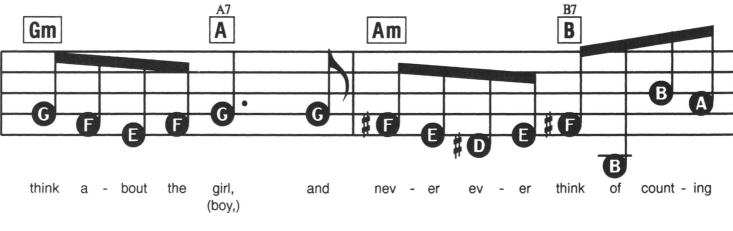

think a - bout the girl, and nev - er ev - er think of count - ing
(boy,)

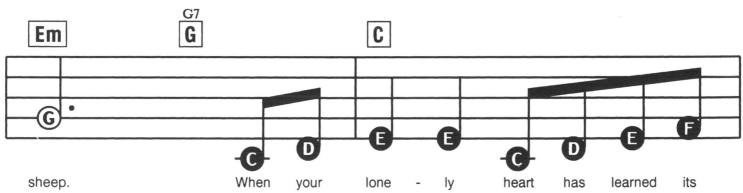

sheep. When your lone - ly heart has learned its

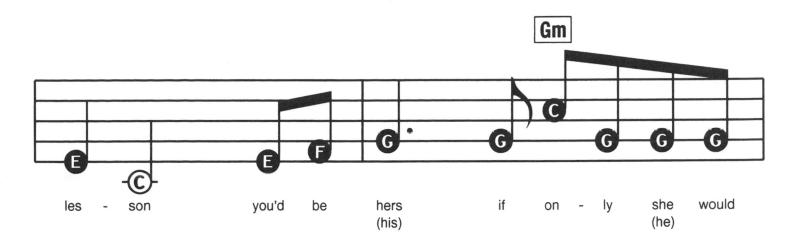

les - son you'd be hers if on - ly she would
(his) (he)

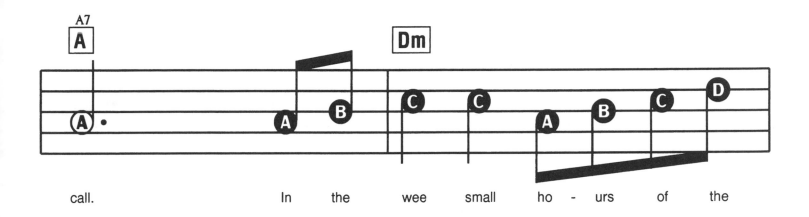

call. In the wee small ho - urs of the

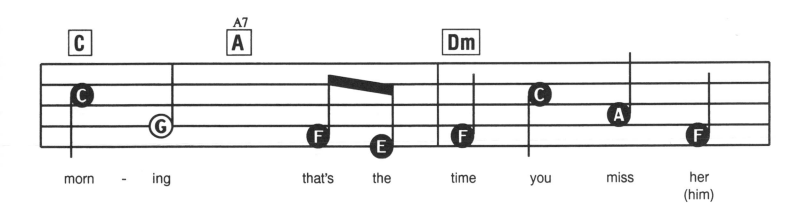

morn - ing that's the time you miss her
(him)

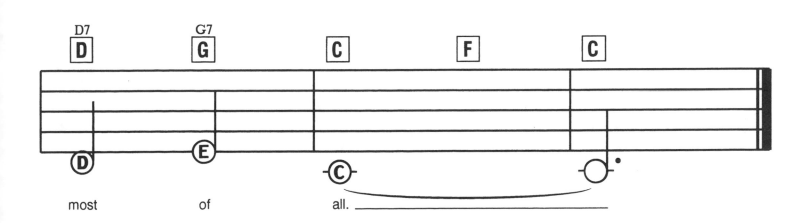

most of all. _____

Gentle Rain
from the Motion Picture THE GENTLE RAIN

Registration 4
Rhythm: Bossa Nova or Latin

Music by Luiz Bonfa
Words by Matt Dubey

Dm A A7

We
I

both are lost
feel your lost tears

and a - lone
as they fall

in the
on my

Cm F F7

world,
cheek,

walk with
they are

me
warm

in the gen - tle
like the gen - tle

B♭ Dm

rain.
rain.

Don't
Come,

be a -
lit - tle

E E7 **Cm** D D7

fraid,
one,

I've a hand
you have me

for your hand,
in the world.

and I
And our

D.C. al Coda
(Return to beginning
Play to ⊕ and
Skip to Coda)

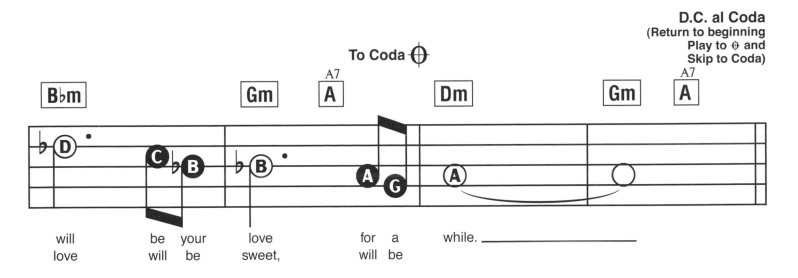

To Coda ⊕

Bbm · · · Gm · A7 A · Dm · Gm · A7 A

will be your love for a while. _____
love will be sweet, will be

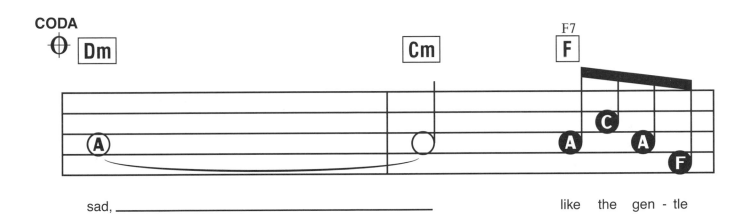

CODA ⊕ Dm · Cm · F7 F

sad, _____ like the gen - tle

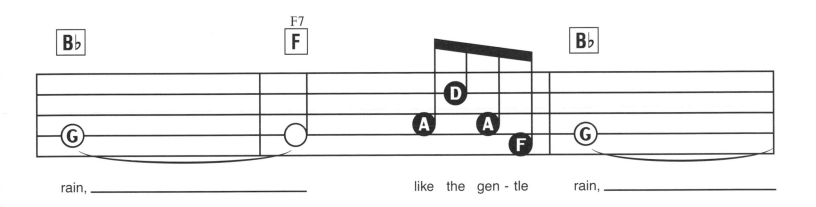

Bb · F7 F · Bb

rain, _____ like the gen - tle rain, _____

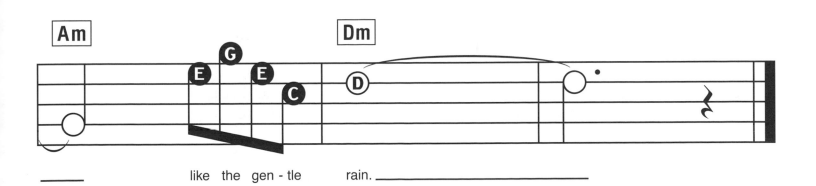

Am · Dm

_____ like the gen - tle rain. _____

If You Go Away

Registration 10
Rhythm: Waltz

French Words and Music by Jacques Brel
English Words by Rod McKuen

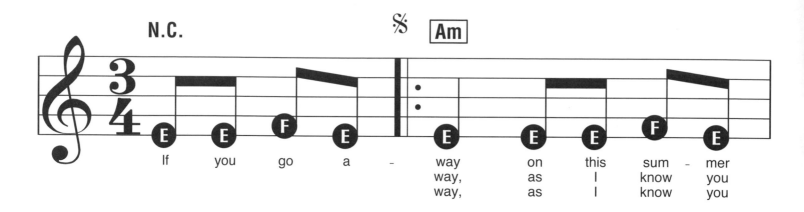

If you go a - way on this sum - mer
way, on as I know you
way, as I know you

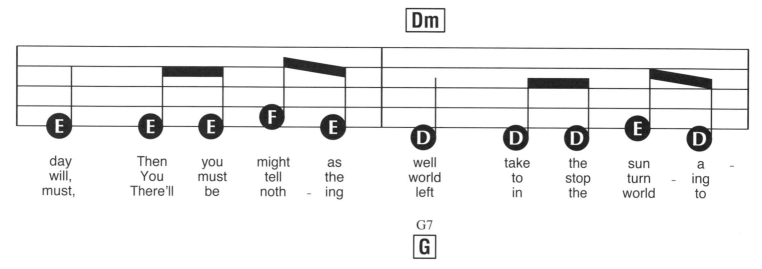

day, Then you might as well take the sun a -
will, You must tell nothing
must, There'll be noth - ing

world left to in the stop turn - ing
world turn to

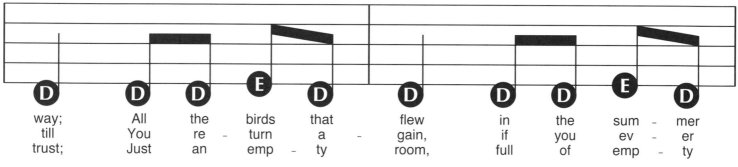

way; All the birds that flew in the sum - mer
till, You re - turn a - gain, if you ev - er
trust; Just an emp - ty room, full of emp - ty

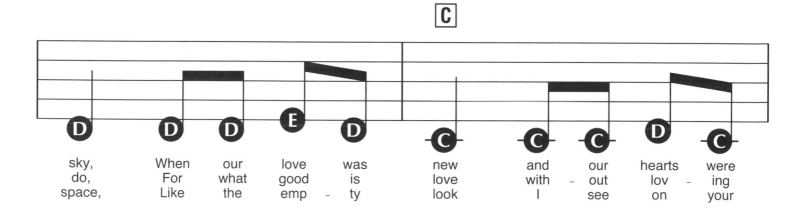

sky, When our love was new and our hearts were
do, For what love good is and with - out lov - ing
space, Like the emp - ty love look I see on your

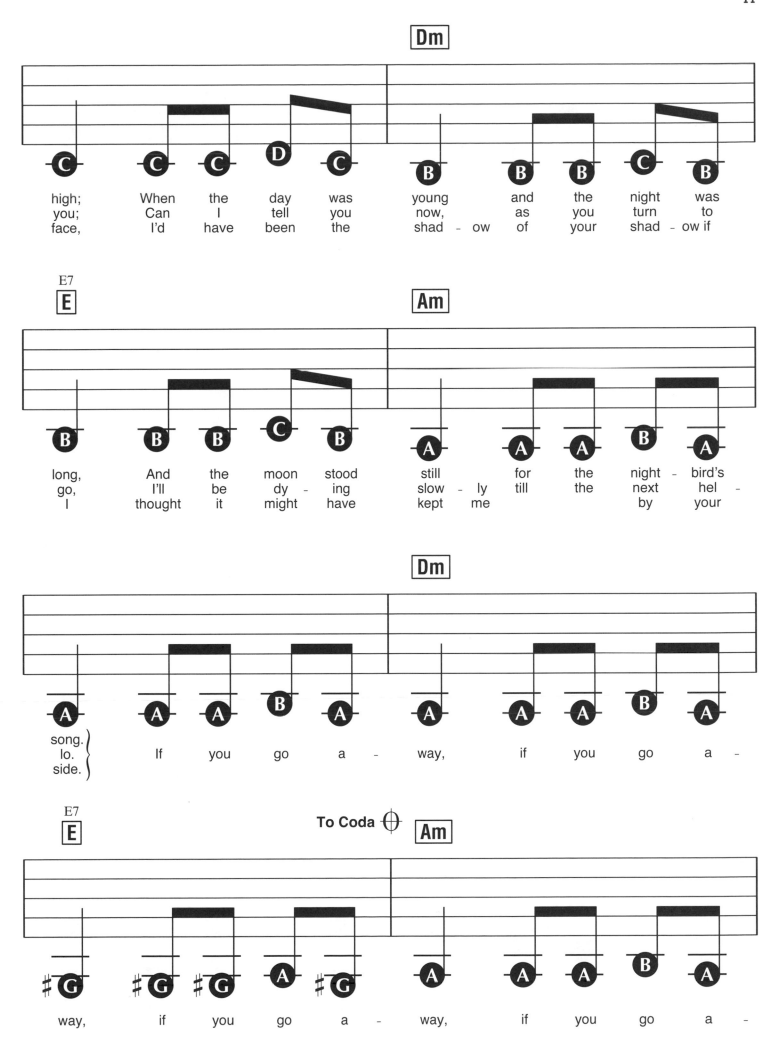

12

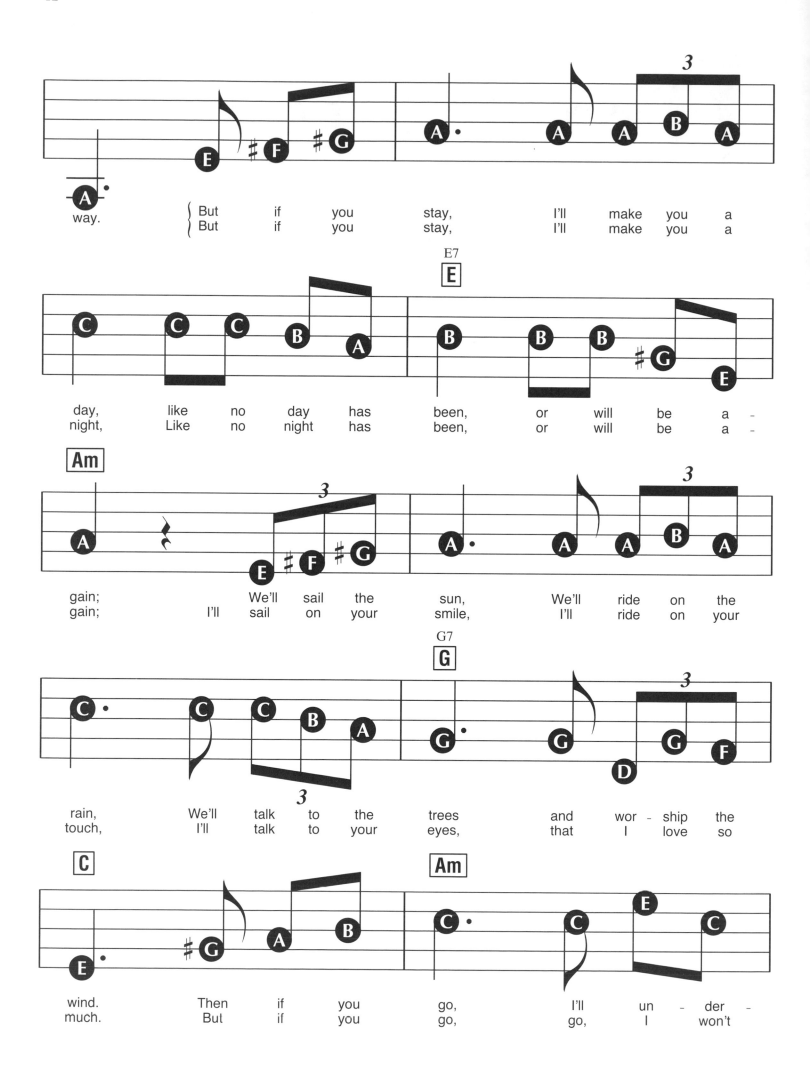

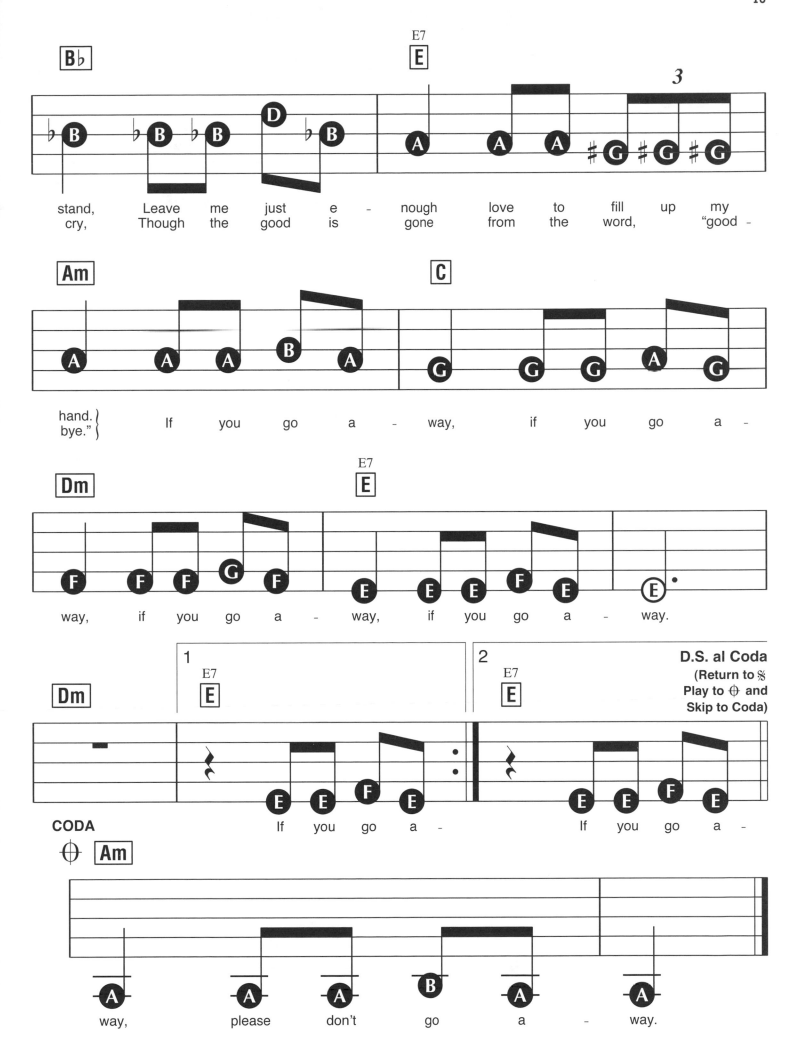

Spring Can Really Hang You Up the Most

Registration 2
Rhythm: Ballad

Lyric by Fran Landesman
Music by Tommy Wolf

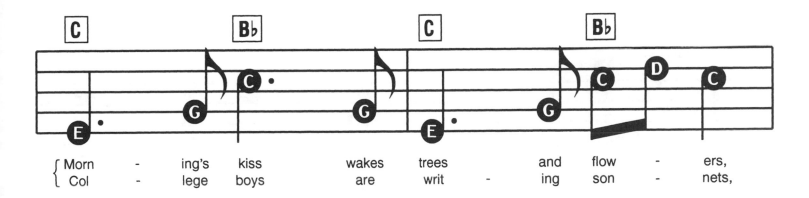

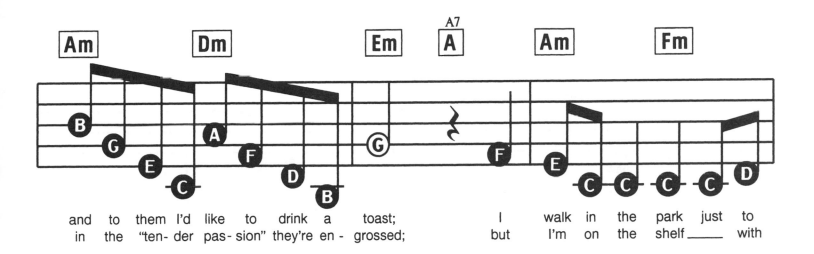

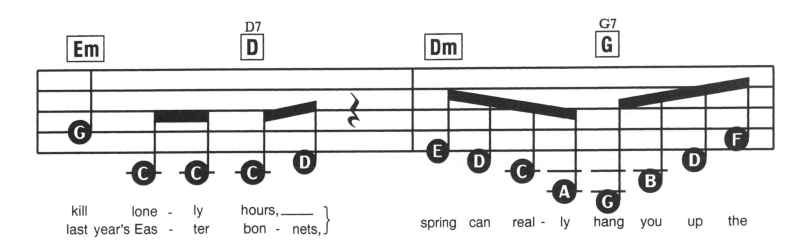

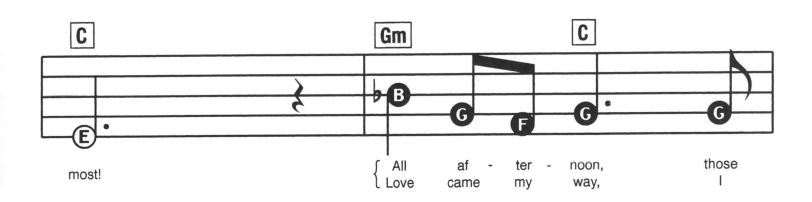

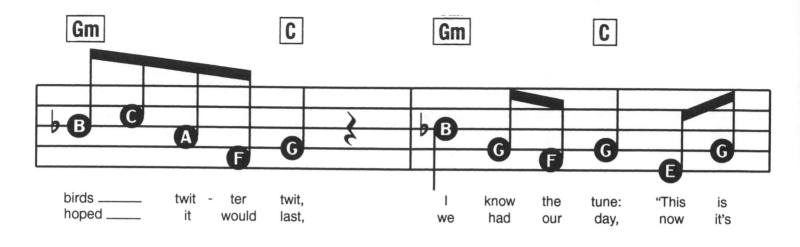

birds _____ twit - ter twit, I know the tune: "This is
hoped _____ it would last, we had our day, now it's

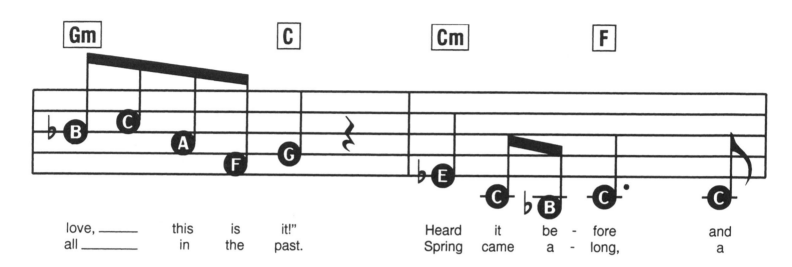

love, _____ this is it!" Heard it be - fore and
all _____ in the past. Spring came a - long, a

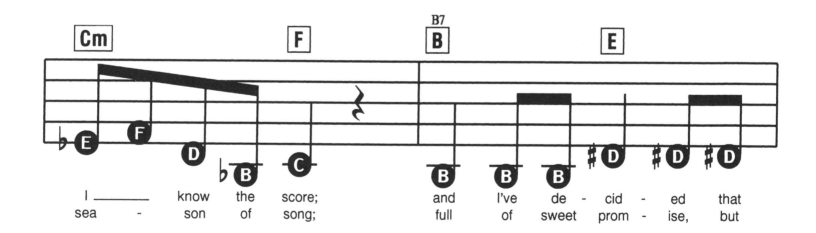

I _____ know the score; and I've de - cid - ed that
sea - son of song; full of sweet prom - ise, but

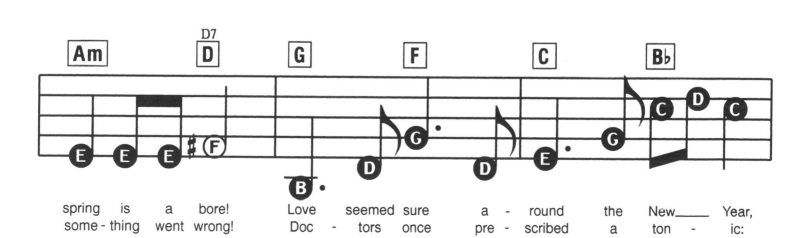

spring is a bore! Love seemed sure a - round the New_____ Year,
some - thing went wrong! Doc - tors once pre - scribed a ton - ic:

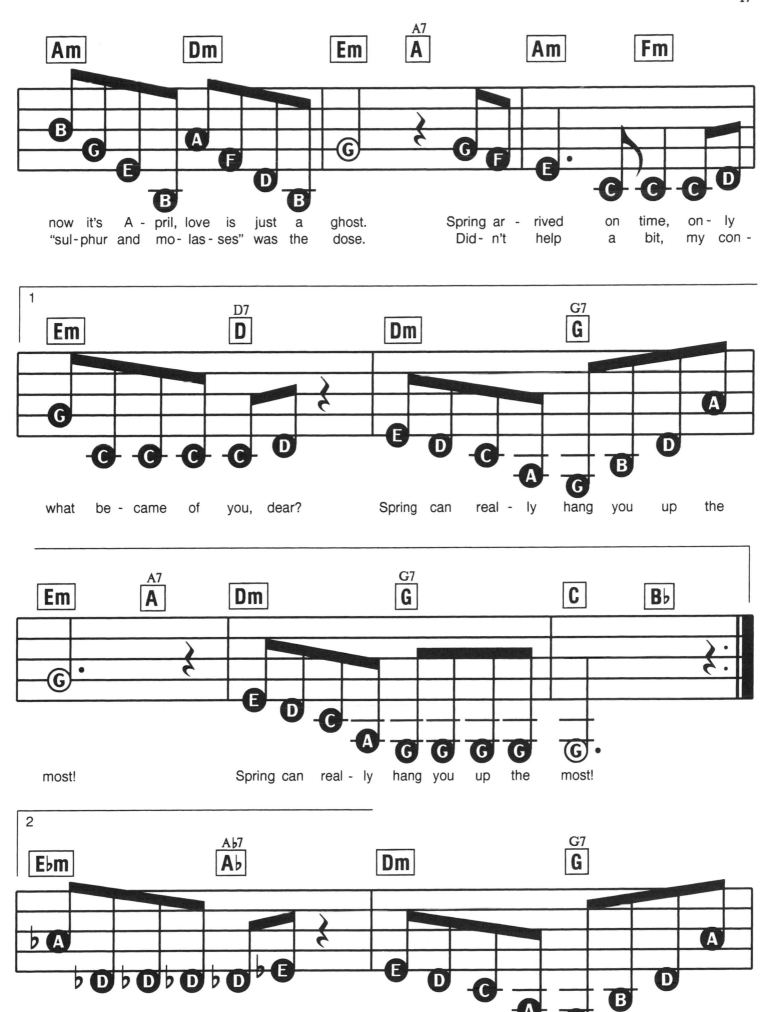

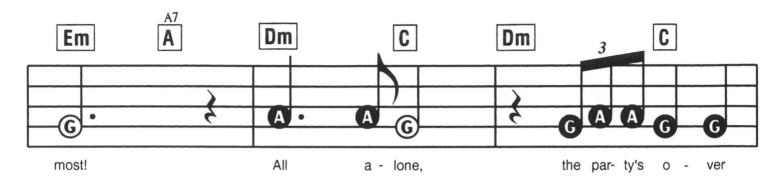

most! All a - lone, the par - ty's o - ver

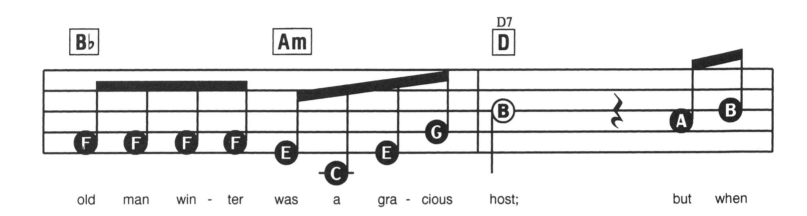

old man win - ter was a gra - cious host; but when

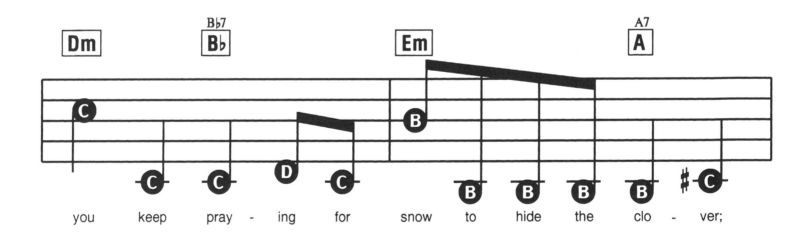

you keep pray - ing for snow to hide the clo - ver;

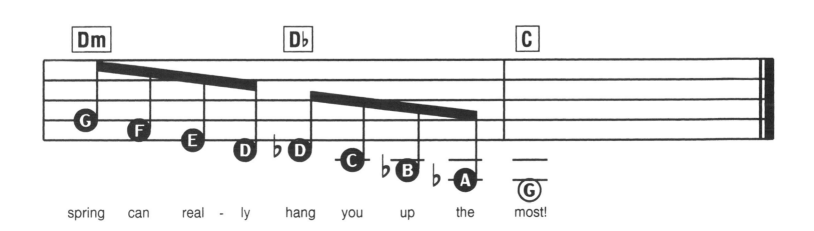

spring can real - ly hang you up the most!

Where Do You Start?

Registration 3
Rhythm: Ballad

Lyric by Alan and Marilyn Bergman
Music by Johnny Mandel

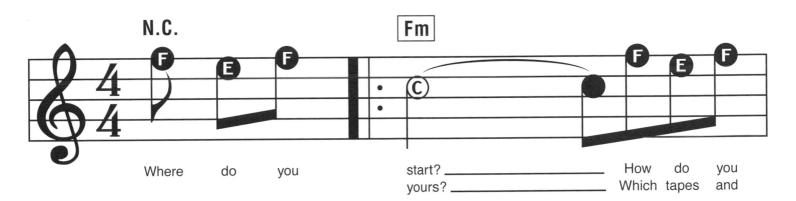

Where do you   start? _____ How do you
yours? _____ Which tapes and

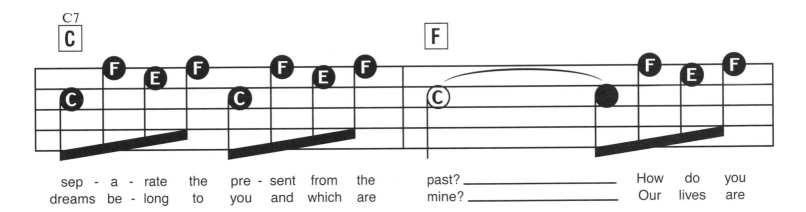

sep - a - rate the pre - sent from the past? _____ How do you
dreams be - long to you and which are mine? _____ Our lives are

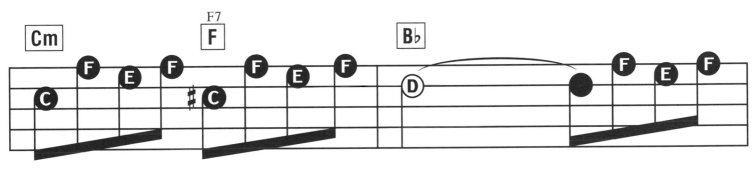

deal with all the things you thought would last, _____ that did - n't
tan - gled like the branch - es of a vine _____ that in - ter -

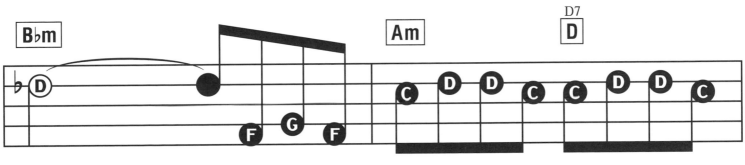

last? _____ With bits of mem - 'ries scat - tered here and there, I
twine. _____ So man - y ha - bits that we'll have to break and

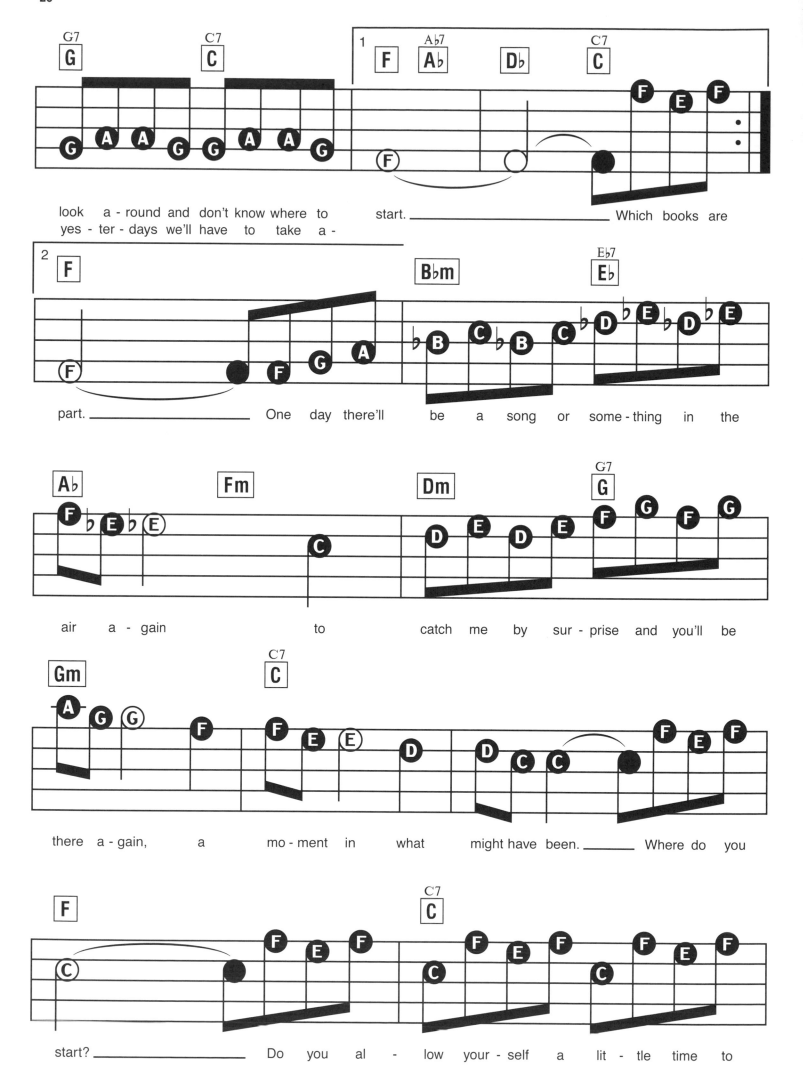

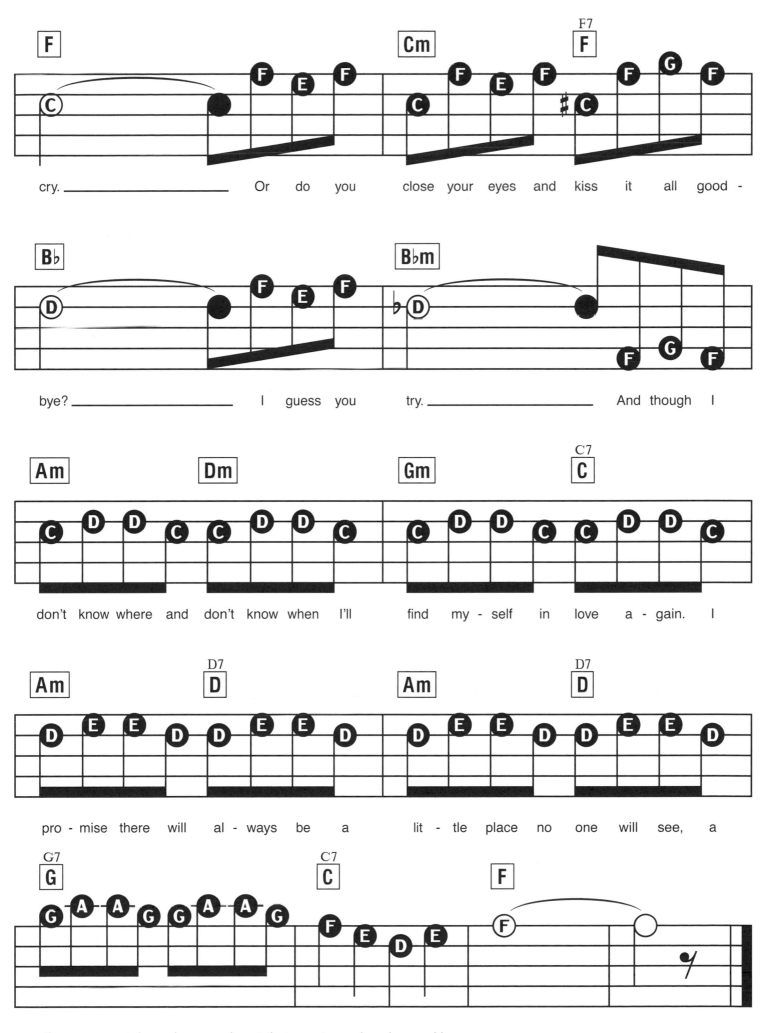

Make Someone Happy
from DO RE MI

Registration 2
Rhythm: Fox Trot or Swing

Words by Betty Comden and Adolph Green
Music by Jule Styne

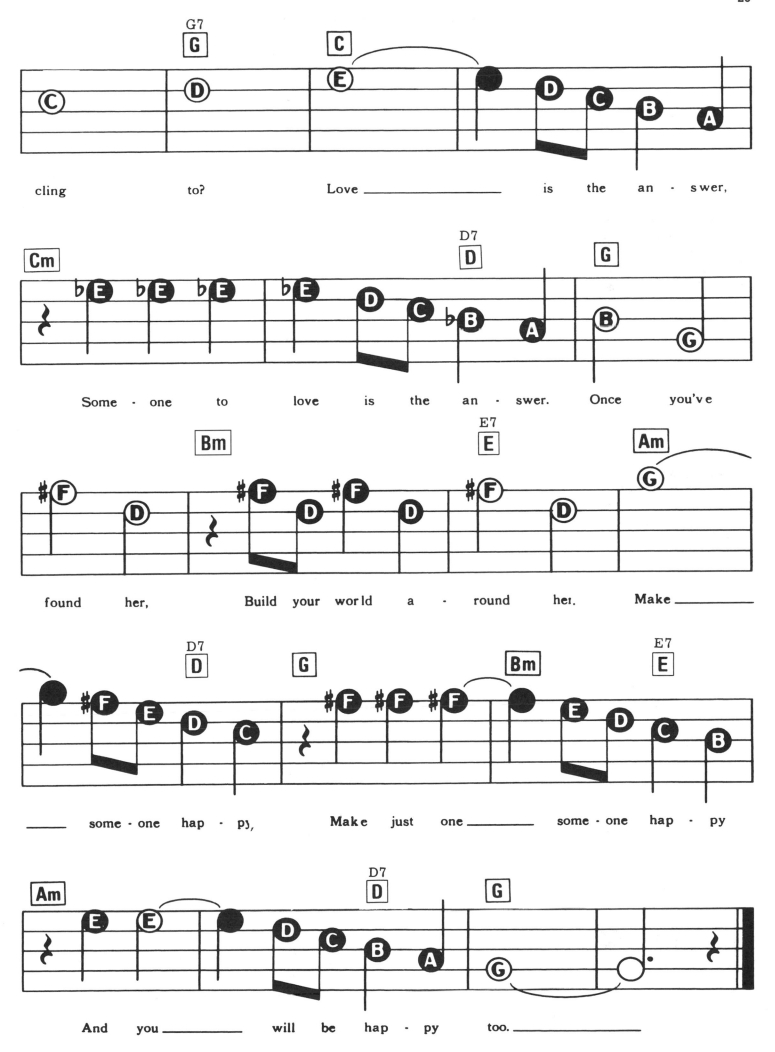

A Time for Love
from AN AMERICAN DREAM

Registration 7
Rhythm: Swing or Jazz

Words by Paul Francis Webster
Music by Johnny Mandel

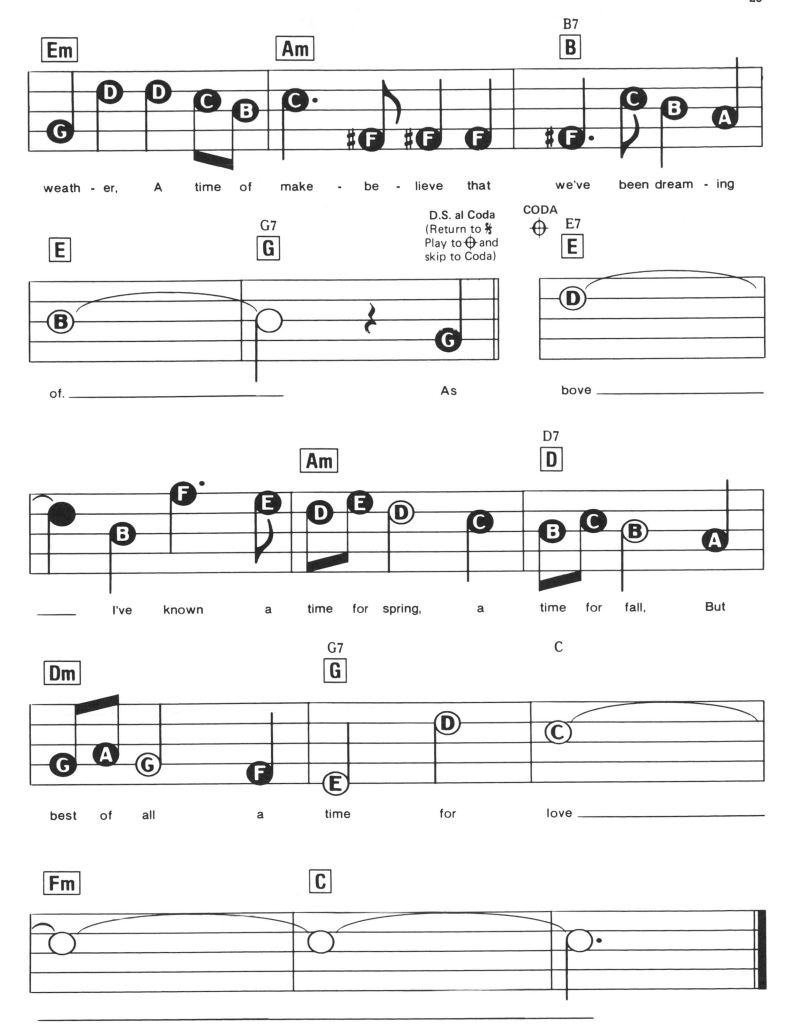

Here's That Rainy Day
from CARNIVAL IN FLANDERS

Registration 2
Rhythm: Ballad or Slow Rock

Words by Johnny Burke
Music by Jimmy Van Heusen

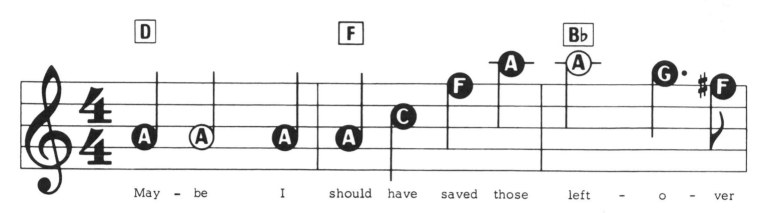

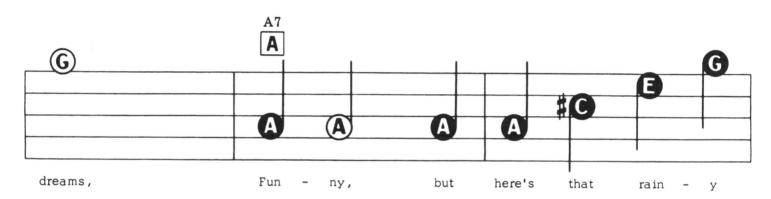

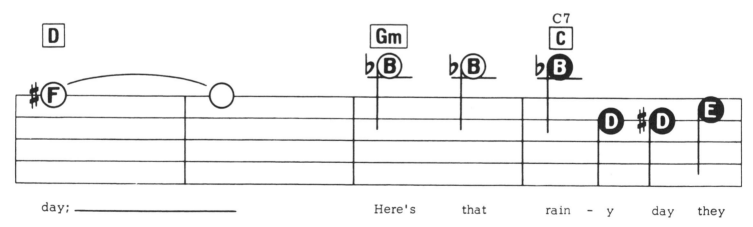

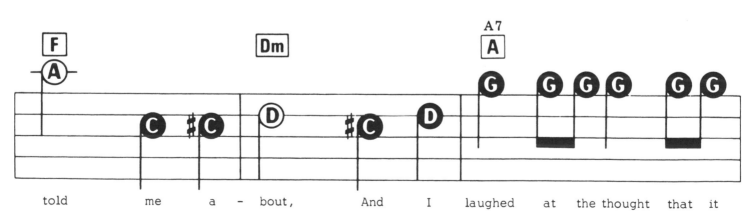

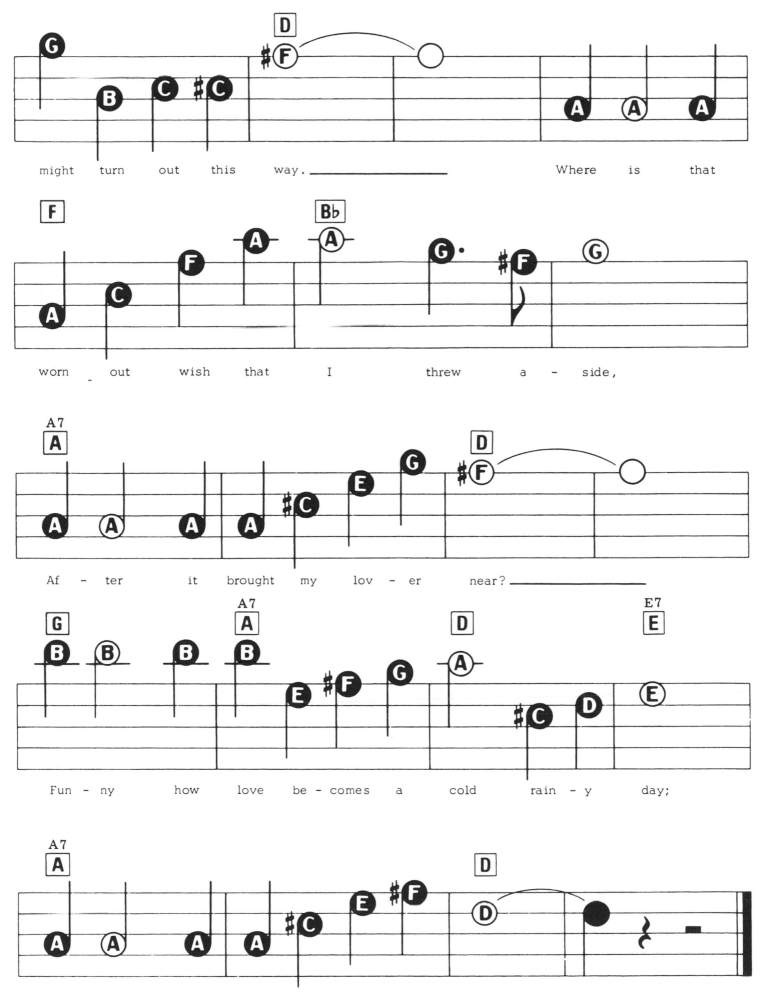

Love Dance

Registration 1
Rhythm: Ballad

Words and Music by Paul H. Williams,
Ivan Guimaraes Lins and Gilson Peranzetta

From too much talk to si - lent touch - es, sweet
We loved, we slept, we left the lights on. The

touch - es.
night's gone

We and turned our morn - ing hearts finds to us love, caught then in

tried it. First time ro - mance,
life's most sen - si - ble trance.

there in the qui - et,
Turn up the qui - et,

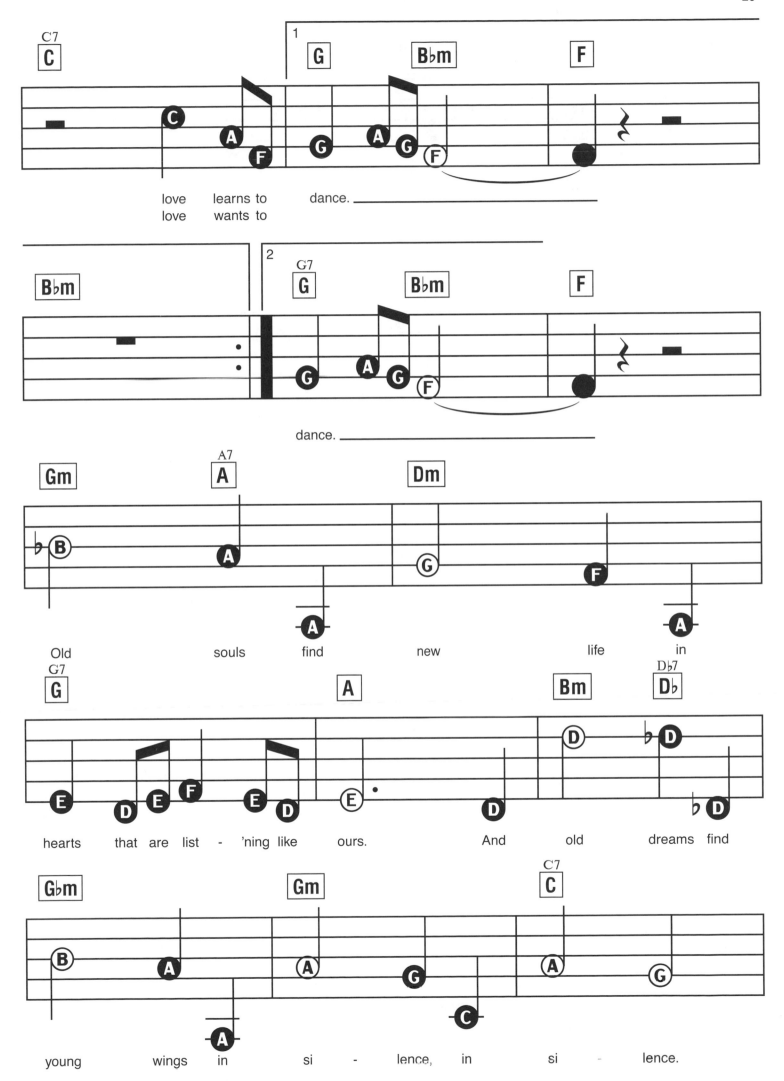

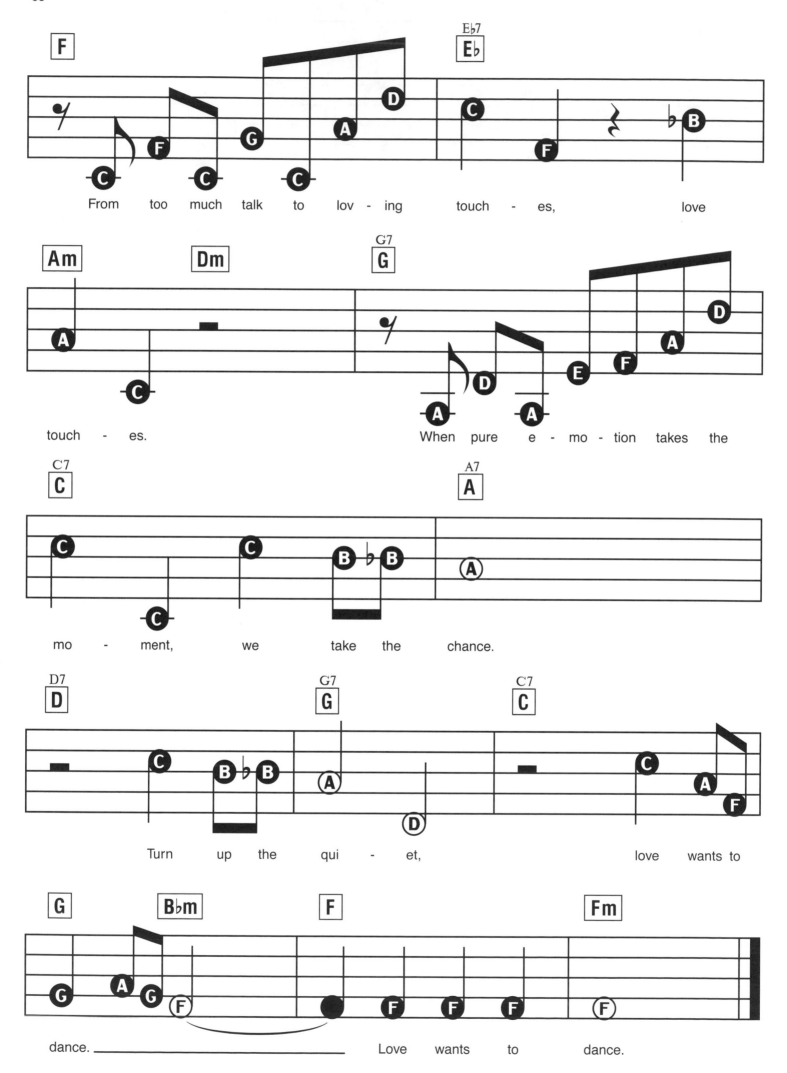

You Must Believe in Spring

Registration 2
Rhythm: Swing

Lyrics by Alan and Marilyn Bergman
Music by Michel Legrand

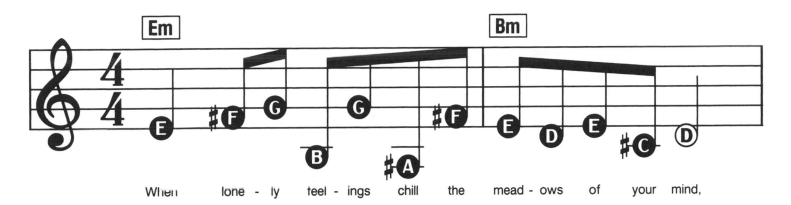

When lone - ly feel - ings chill the mead - ows of your mind,

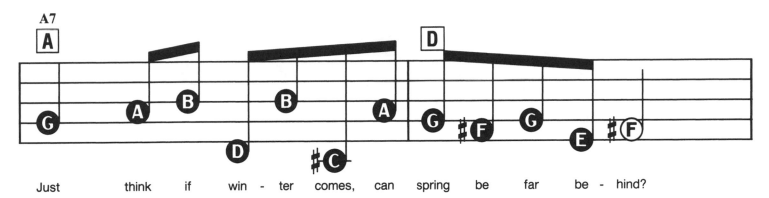

Just think if win - ter comes, can spring be far be - hind?

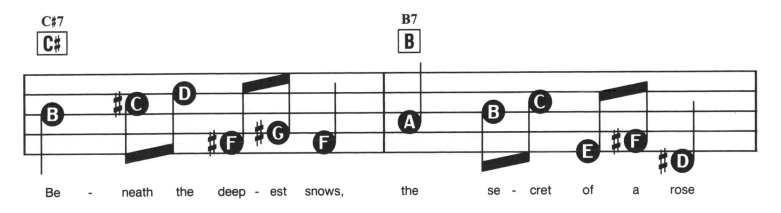

Be - neath the deep - est snows, the se - cret of a rose

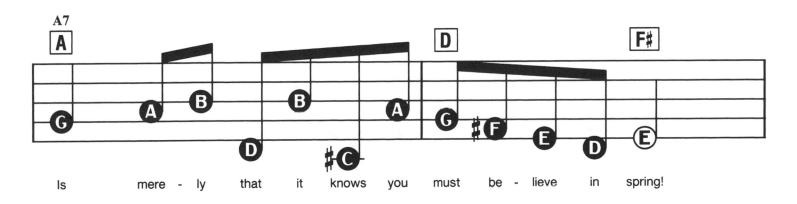

Is mere - ly that it knows you must be - lieve in spring!

32

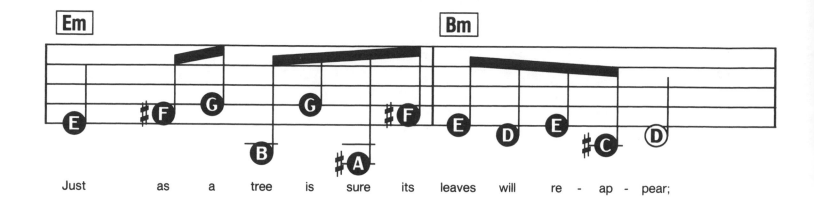

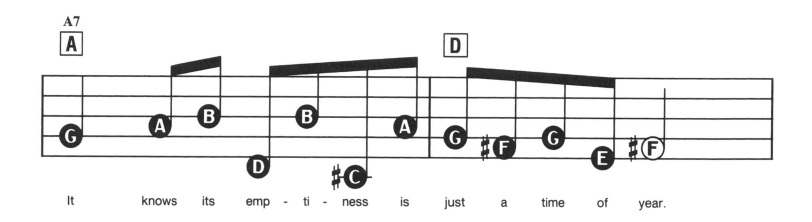

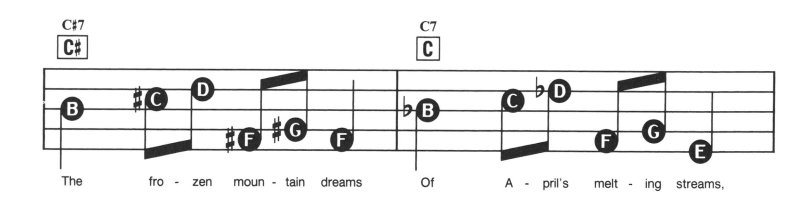

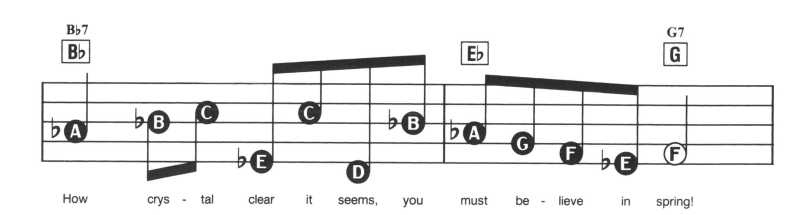

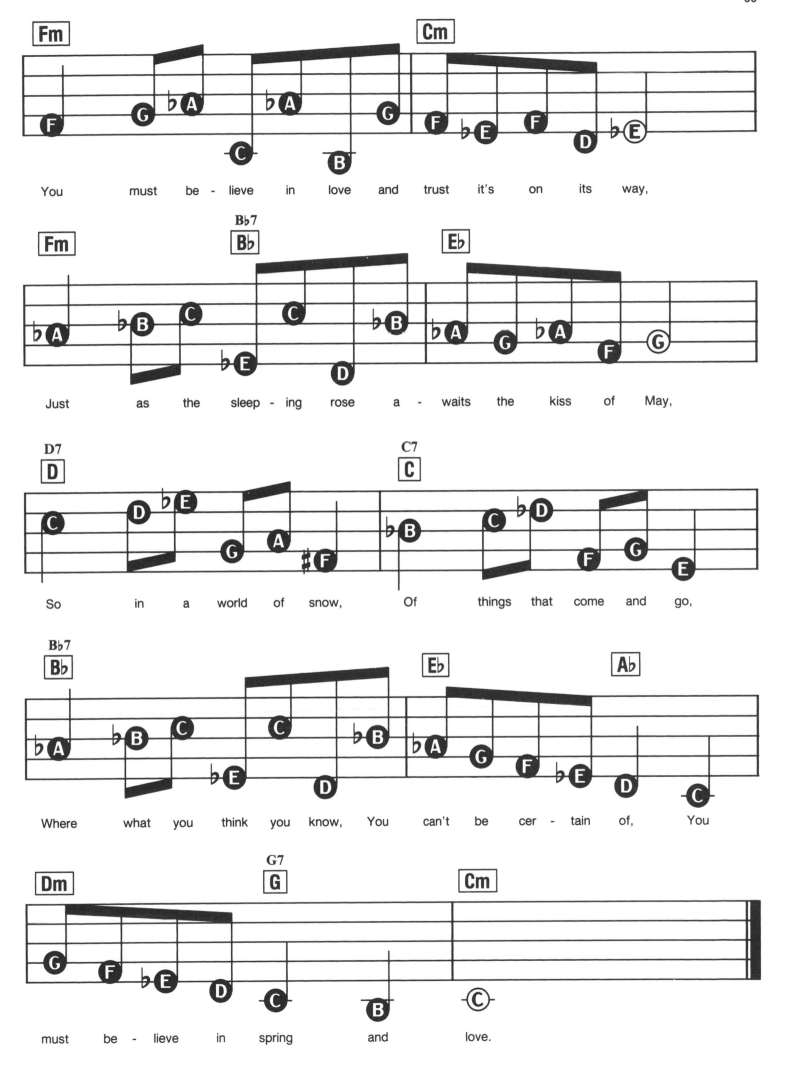

Smoke Gets in Your Eyes
from ROBERTA

Registration 10
Rhythm: Ballad or Swing

Words by Otto Harbach
Music by Jerome Kern

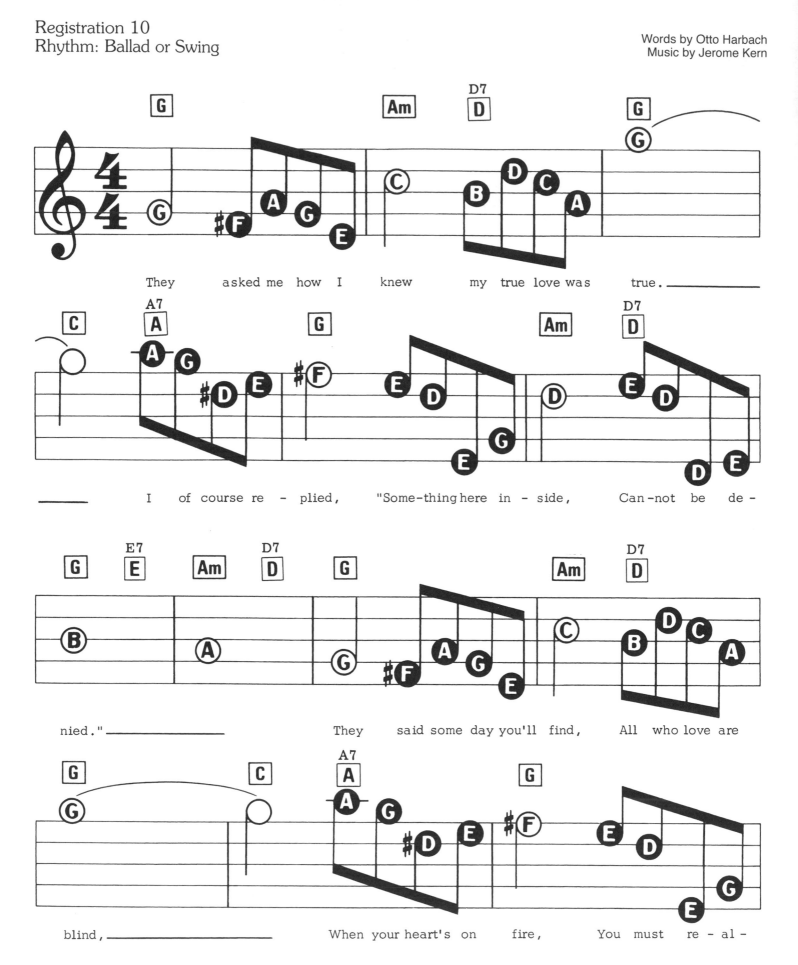

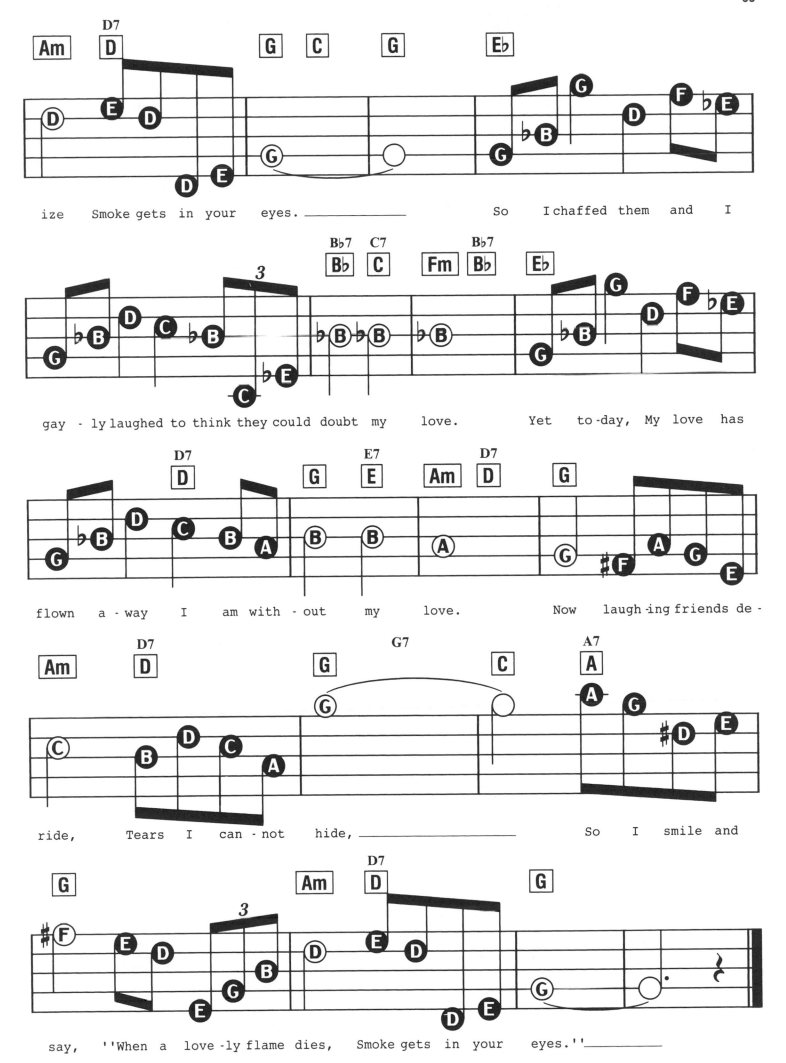

Some Other Time
from ON THE TOWN

Registration 3
Rhythm: Ballad or Fox Trot

Music by Leonard Bernstein
Lyrics by Betty Comden and Adolph Green

Where has the time all gone to?
This day was just a to - ken.

Have - n't done half the things we want to.
Too man - y words are still un - spo - ken.

Oh, well, we'll catch up some oth - er time.

oth - er time. _____ Just when the fun is

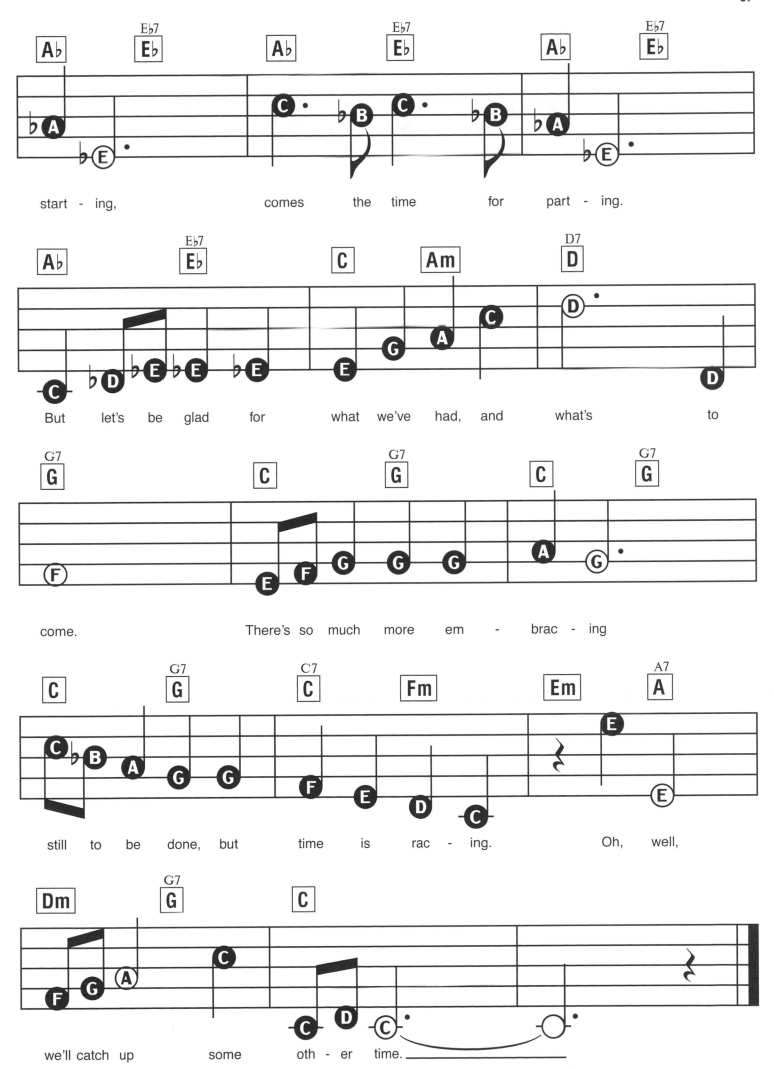

Registration Guide

- Match the Registration number on the song to the corresponding numbered category below. Select and activate an instrumental sound available on your instrument.

- Choose an automatic rhythm appropriate to the mood and style of the song. (Consult your Owner's Guide for proper operation of automatic rhythm features.)

- Adjust the tempo and volume controls to comfortable settings.

Registration

1	Mellow	Flutes, Clarinet, Oboe, Flugel Horn, Trombone, French Horn, Organ Flutes
2	Ensemble	Brass Section, Sax Section, Wind Ensemble, Full Organ, Theater Organ
3	Strings	Violin, Viola, Cello, Fiddle, String Ensemble, Pizzicato, Organ Strings
4	Guitars	Acoustic/Electric Guitars, Banjo, Mandolin, Dulcimer, Ukulele, Hawaiian Guitar
5	Mallets	Vibraphone, Marimba, Xylophone, Steel Drums, Bells, Celesta, Chimes
6	Liturgical	Pipe Organ, Hand Bells, Vocal Ensemble, Choir, Organ Flutes
7	Bright	Saxophones, Trumpet, Mute Trumpet, Synth Leads, Jazz/Gospel Organs
8	Piano	Piano, Electric Piano, Honky Tonk Piano, Harpsichord, Clavi
9	Novelty	Melodic Percussion, Wah Trumpet, Synth, Whistle, Kazoo, Perc. Organ
10	Bellows	Accordion, French Accordion, Mussette, Harmonica, Pump Organ, Bagpipes

More Great Piano/Vocal Books

FROM CHERRY LANE

For a complete listing of Cherry Lane titles available, including contents listings, please visit our web site at

www.cherrylane.com

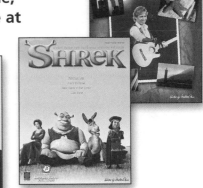
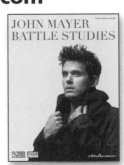

More Big-Note & Easy Piano Books

For a complete listing of Cherry Lane titles available, including contents listings, please visit our web site at www.cherrylane.com

CLASSICAL CHRISTMAS

Easy solo arrangements of 30 wonderful holiday songs: Ave Maria • Dance of the Sugar Plum Fairy • Evening Prayer • Gesu Bambino • Hallelujah! • He Shall Feed His Flock • March of the Toys • O Come, All Ye Faithful • O Holy Night • Pastoral Symphony • Sheep May Safely Graze • Sinfonia • Waltz of the Flowers • and more.
___02500112 Easy Piano Solo $9.95

BEST OF JOHN DENVER

A collection of 18 Denver classics, including: Leaving on a Jet Plane • Take Me Home, Country Roads • Rocky Mountain High • Follow Me • and more.
___02505512 Easy Piano $9.95

JOHN DENVER ANTHOLOGY

Easy arrangements of 34 of the finest from this beloved artist. Includes: Annie's Song • Fly Away • Follow Me • Grandma's Feather Bed • Leaving on a Jet Plane • Perhaps Love • Rocky Mountain High • Sunshine on My Shoulders • Take Me Home, Country Roads • Thank God I'm a Country Boy • and many more.
___02501366 Easy Piano $19.99

DOWN THE AISLE

Easy piano arrangements of 20 beloved pop and classical wedding songs, including: Air on the G String • Ave Maria • Canon in D • Follow Me • Give Me Forever (I Do) • Jesu, Joy of Man's Desiring • Prince of Denmark's March • Through the Years • Trumpet Tune • Unchained Melody • Wedding March • When I Fall in Love • You Decorated My Life • and more.
___025000267 Easy Piano $9.95

EASY BROADWAY SHOWSTOPPERS

Easy piano arrangements of 16 traditional and new Broadway standards, including: "Impossible Dream" from *Man of La Mancha* • "Unusual Way" from *Nine* • "This Is the Moment" from *Jekyll & Hyde* • many more.
___02505517 Easy Piano $12.95

A FAMILY CHRISTMAS AROUND THE PIANO

25 songs for hours of family fun, including: Away in a Manger • Deck the Hall • The First Noel • God Rest Ye Merry, Gentlemen • Hark! the Herald Angels Sing • Jingle Bells • Jolly Old St. Nicholas • Joy to the World • O Little Town of Bethlehem • Silent Night, Holy Night • The Twelve Days of Christmas • and more.
___02500398 Easy Piano $7.95

FAVORITE CELTIC SONGS FOR EASY PIANO

Easy arrangements of 40 Celtic classics, including: The Ash Grove • The Bluebells of Scotland • A Bunch of Thyme • Danny Boy • Finnegan's Wake • I'll Tell Me Ma • Loch Lomond • My Wild Irish Rose • The Rose of Tralee • and more!
___02501306 Easy Piano $12.99

FAVORITE POP BALLADS

This new collection features 35 beloved ballads, including: Breathe (2 AM) • Faithfully • Leaving on a Jet Plane • Open Arms • Ordinary People • Summer Breeze • These Eyes • Truly • You've Got a Friend • and more.
___02501005 Easy Piano $15.99

HOLY CHRISTMAS CAROLS COLORING BOOK

A terrific songbook with 7 sacred carols and lots of coloring pages for the young pianist. Songs include: Angels We Have Heard on High • The First Noel • Hark! The Herald Angels Sing • It Came upon a Midnight Clear • O Come All Ye Faithful • O Little Town of Bethlehem • Silent Night.
___02500277 Five-Finger Piano $6.95

JEKYLL & HYDE – VOCAL SELECTIONS

Ten songs from the Wildhorn/Bricusse Broadway smash, arranged for big-note: In His Eyes • It's a Dangerous Game • Lost in the Darkness • A New Life • No One Knows Who I Am • Once Upon a Dream • Someone Like You • Sympathy, Tenderness • Take Me as I Am • This Is the Moment.
___02500023 Big-Note Piano $9.95

JACK JOHNSON ANTHOLOGY

Easy arrangements of 27 of the best from this Hawaiian singer/songwriter, including: Better Together • Breakdown • Flake • Fortunate Fool • Good People • Sitting, Waiting, Wishing • Taylor • and more.
___02501313 Easy Piano $19.99

JUST FOR KIDS – NOT! CHRISTMAS SONGS

This unique collection of 14 Christmas favorites is fun for the whole family! Kids can play the full-sounding big-note solos alone, or with their parents (or teachers) playing accompaniment for the thrill of four-hand piano! Includes: Deck the Halls • Jingle Bells • Silent Night • What Child Is This? • and more.
___02505510 Big-Note Piano $8.95

JUST FOR KIDS – NOT! CLASSICS

Features big-note arrangements of classical masterpieces, plus optional accompaniment for adults. Songs: Air on the G String • Dance of the Sugar Plum Fairy • Für Elise • Jesu, Joy of Man's Desiring • Ode to Joy • Pomp and Circumstance • The Sorcerer's Apprentice • William Tell Overture • and more!
___02505513 Classics....................$7.95
___02500301 More Classics $8.95

JUST FOR KIDS – NOT! FUN SONGS

Fun favorites for kids everywhere in big-note arrangements for piano, including: Bingo • Eensy Weensy Spider • Farmer in the Dell • Jingle Bells • London Bridge • Pop Goes the Weasel • Puff the Magic Dragon • Skip to My Lou • Twinkle, Twinkle Little Star • and more!
___02505523 Fun Songs................$7.95

JUST FOR KIDS – NOT! TV THEMES & MOVIE SONGS

Entice the kids to the piano with this delightful collection of songs and themes from movies and TV. These big-note arrangements include themes from The Brady Bunch and The Addams Family, as well as Do-Re-Mi (The Sound of Music), theme from Beetlejuice (Day-O) and Puff the Magic Dragon. Each song includes an accompaniment part for teacher or adult so that the kids can experience the joy of four-hand playing as well! Plus performance tips.
___02505507 TV Themes & Movie Songs $9.95
___02500304 More TV Themes & Movie Songs $9.95

MERRY CHRISTMAS, EVERYONE

Over 20 contemporary and classic all-time holiday favorites arranged for big-note piano or easy piano. Includes: Away in a Manger • Christmas Like a Lullaby • The First Noel • Joy to the World • The Marvelous Toy • and more.
___02505600 Big-Note Piano $9.95

POKEMON 2 B.A. MASTER

This great songbook features easy piano arrangements of 13 tunes from the hit TV series: 2.B.A. Master • Double Trouble (Team Rocket) • Everything Changes • Misty's Song • My Best Friends • Pokémon (Dance Mix) • Pokémon Theme • PokéRAP • The Time Has Come (Pikachu's Goodbye) • Together, Forever • Viridian City • What Kind of Pokémon Are You? • You Can Do It (If You Really Try). Includes a full-color, 8-page pull-out section featuring characters and scenes from this super hot show.
___02500145 Easy Piano $12.95

POP/ROCK LOVE SONGS

Easy arrangements of 18 romatic favorites, including: Always • Bed of Roses • Butterfly Kisses • Follow Me • From This Moment On • Hard Habit to Break • Leaving on a Jet Plane • When You Say Nothing at All • more.
___02500151 Easy Piano $10.95

POPULAR CHRISTMAS CAROLS COLORING BOOK

Kids are sure to love this fun holiday songbook! It features five-finger piano arrangements of seven Christmas classics, complete with coloring pages throughout! Songs include: Deck the Hall • Good King Wenceslas • Jingle Bells • Jolly Old St. Nicholas • O Christmas Tree • Up on the Housetop • We Wish You a Merry Christmas.
___02500276 Five-Finger Piano $6.95

PUFF THE MAGIC DRAGON & 54 OTHER ALL-TIME CHILDREN'S FAVORITESONGS

55 timeless songs enjoyed by generations of kids, and sure to be favorites for years to come. Songs include: A-Tisket A-Tasket • Alouette • Eensy Weensy Spider • The Farmer in the Dell • I've Been Working on the Railroad • If You're Happy and You Know It • Joy to the World • Michael Finnegan • Oh Where, Oh Where Has My Little Dog Gone • Silent Night • Skip to My Lou • This Old Man • and many more.
___02500017 Big-Note Piano $12.95

See your local music dealer or contact:

 cherry lane music company

 HAL•LEONARD®
EXCLUSIVELY DISTRIBUTED BY
7777 W. BLUEMOUND RD. P.O. BOX 13819 MILWAUKEE, WI 53213

Prices, contents, and availability subject to change without notice.

0710